STRAIGHT

from the

HEART

Barbara Jean Woodson

ISBN 978-1-0980-1246-5 (paperback)
ISBN 978-1-0980-1247-2 (digital)

Christian Faith Publishing, Inc.
832 Park Avenue
Meadville, PA 16335
www.christianfaithpublishing.com

Printed in the United States of America

Contents

AMERICA

M omma
said there would be days like this
life
is what You make of it
many decisions
will play a part
make them with both Your mind and heart
It's okay to stand
for what You believe
but
don't wear hate
upon Your sleeve
Black,
Brown, and White
are crayons
in a box they belong
not
in Gang wars
to right a wrong
God
Bless America
let
prayer
carry from Our churches
to the Schools
put
His words above the rules
America

Red, White, and Blue
enough
blood has been shed on You
let's
rise above
all of Us
trade destruction for God's love

An Angel

*T*here's no mo' rain
"Thank God
'cause you're not dead"
He took My hand
that held My head
as I sat on the edge of the curb
the softest voice said

As
I glanced up
a light was shining upon a face
of a child
with big eyes and a gentle smile
speaking words of a wise soul
couldn't have been no more
than five or six years old

Standing
on his bare feet
this is what He said to Me
I
felt the waters
freezing My toes
coming into My nose
Momma
said close your eyes baby
it's going to be okay
know that God is with Us

Tears
streamed down My face
his small hand
wiped them away
causing a breath of life
to race through My heart
He was right
no
broken bones nor scars
As
I turned the boy had gone
An Angel
leaving My life to carry on

AMERICAN WAY

*J*ust
the other Day
I
heard a husband say
the fellows called Me
a weak Man
'cause
I rely on a group
of strong Women
But
I don't care
for the strength I'm receiving
keeps Me believing
it won't be long
Well
unlike You
My dreams keep me awake
and
I find Myself drowning in fear
of being left alone
I
wish My Husband was here
have
an answer to when Mom is coming home
No
matter how hard I try
without telling a lie
tears still fill

Their curious eyes
We
all got to keep holding on
drawing
from each other's faith
shall keep Us strong
So
tie yellow ribbons
around the oak trees
Fly
American flags
as high
that the wind allows them to be
But
before the night folds
and
Our tired minds
tuck in Our weary Souls
don't forget to pray
for
Your loved ones return home
the American way

BIG GIRLS NEED LOVE TOO

I
know that when You glance at Me
all you see
is a Woman on swollen feet
have you ever thought
to take the time to
seek
what's really deep inside

Besides
the largeness of Me
see My beautiful face
tender heart
always in the right place
when
I say I love You
truly I do

Everyone
needs someone
to hold
one to a life grow old
pointing and staring
used to bring Me down
Prayer
kept Me on solid ground
Faith
is the hope that lets
Me know a love will be found

The
next time Our paths cross ways
hello
would be the thing to do
as your eyes meet mine
'cause
big Girls need love too

BRING BACK THE LAUGHTER

*T*here's
a small town
North of Laredo
They
finally put it on the map
If
You've never been there
chances are
You won't find where it's at
We'd
laugh till We cry
this was the place to be
playing ball
with the hot sand
burning beneath Our feet
Hanging
a garden hose from a cypress tree
was a joy of Mine
bathing by the moonlight
in the summertime
Nothing
like lying on an old cot
listening
to the water running
through the rocks
I
like riding horse back
to a secret place

with a cool breeze
blowing across My face
Now
Everyone has up and moved away
not
much left to make them stay
but
I hold to what Grandpa said
to Me
don't give up on the Human race
please
not in this place
those were the good ol' days
I
still long after
wish
I
knew how to bring back the laughter

CAMPUS GROUNDS

I
don't know
what You were thinking
it just wasn't right
to make a decision
in taking so many lives
leaving hallways
echoing in pain
We
can point fingers at Your Mother
lay blame upon Your Father
go deep
into Your Family's history
it won't bring back those close to Me
They'll
read all Your journals
try to recognize the signals
but
no one will truly understand
the dark side of an angry Man
Every time
another school goes down
memories from the last one
comes back around
opening
wounds of broken hearts
from when their lives
were torn apart

Our Children
one day are Heaven bound
not
through death on campus grounds
"Stop
the bloodshed everywhere
and
let God be the one
that takes them there"

Country Girl

I
wasn't born
on the night of a new Moon
or
draped in raw silk
or
have never eaten from a sliver spoon
All
I know of riches and gold
were from the stories My Grandpa told
My
Saturdays were spent cleaning
the ol' Church
listening
to Grandpa preach on how hard work don't hurt
Just
a small-Town Girl
city lights
brought God into My World
Forgiven
Me of My past
future built on faith
through prayer will make it last
I'm
just a county Girl
on bended knees
to You, Lord, giving all of Me

Don't Take Away My Baby

I said
I would change
wait let Me explain
I'm
not in the streets no more
I know what I'm living for
You said
if I got a job I did
darn good one too
I
stop doing drugs
can't see the tracks like You used to
If You
take away My life
with all the love She gives
You leave Me with no reason to live
God,
don't let them destroy
this precious flower
putting Her among Strangers
to poke and stare
there's no greater love than Ours
We've become one
She belongs with Me
Our
lives have just begun
see it be in Your hearts
don't tear Us apart

Please,
Mr. Man, and, Ms. Lady,
don't take away My Baby

DAD

*P*ride
had separated Us
allowing time to pass on by
now here I am once again
having to say goodbye
Though
years have come and gone
can't
help looking back
at the night that went so wrong
I
often find Myself
sitting by Your graveside
needing to talk to You
just
to say what I've been up to
Sorry
is the only word
I
say a thousand times
God,
help My exhausted mind
Tragedy
can slip on in
closing doors
Sons,
don't be a Day late
or

dollar short
"Love
Your Fathers,"
says the Lord
This
World can get me
Sidetracked
life's woes
hanging on My back
But
sometimes I feel a nudge
I
know it's You,
Dad,
giving Me a hug

Don't Slip Away

*Y*ou
may hear someone calling
it's Me
I'm
the one in need
but
You don't move
for the sadness
entwined Your aches and pain
leaving
Your mind standing still
not
hearing Me call Your name
As
I look into Your eyes
it's as though You're not here
this illness
has taken You elsewhere
the
Little ones
don't understand
why
Their hugs
have no return
of Your loving hands
wake up
don't
slip further into darkness

shed
some tears and cry
help Me
fight for Your life
"Momma,
open Your heart
don't slip away
please
hear the words I pray
wanting and asking
God
to heal You today"

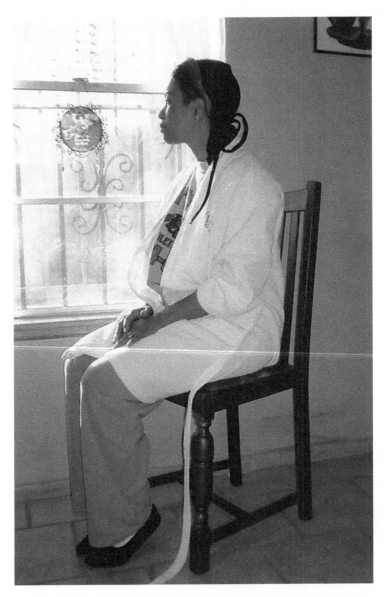

FAMILY THERAPY

I
refuse to lie in bed
let negative thoughts
run through My head
So
thank You, Doc,
for all You give
But
I
won't allow
You to tell Me
how long I have to live
chemo
might be okay
but
not for Me today
can't bear watching Folks'
loved ones slip away
That's
why I'm going home
for
Momma's love to fuel Me
Daddy' s
arms will hold Me
Family and Friends
remind Me
just how Blessed I've been
Sure

I'd trade it all
for a second chance
and
if possible
not to be told My life will end
You
see time of every minute
that
I have of it
is
what God sees will be
in My heart
No doubt
good ol'-fashioned
Family therapy

Good Bones

*T*here's
not even a notion
that someone
would place it on a cliff
overlooking the ocean
and
it's alright by Me
'Cause
what You don't know
is that the sweat and tears
fell upon the mortar
and formed the stone
While
His strength was pulled from above
Morning till night covered in God's love
His
faith framed in the walls
ceiling to floor
Through
broken windows
I
saw uneven doors
welcoming
Strangers who are Friends
making
Family history without an end
Creaking
stairs tell a story

listen with Your heart
in all its glory
this house won't fall apart
You
can't put a price on this ol' home
for there aren't many built
not any
with good ol' bones

I'm Just a Baby

$\mathcal{Y}$ou
are to hold me gently
squeeze Me softly
lift Me with love
Speak
to Me in a low voice
no
need to shout
I'm gonna cry
God
gave You patience
you'll
figure Me out
My
heart must not skip a beat
a scrambled mind
won't be complete
for a beaten soul
will stay asleep
If
anger hangs on to You
shake it off
leave it at the door
broken bones
I don't need
When
feeling frustrated
it

doesn't have to be all on You
leave Me on the steps
of a fire station
They'll know what to do
Sounds
a little crazy
but
it's just Me
saving You
'cause I'm just a Baby

LET YOUR STORY BE TOLD

*G*randma,
tell Me 'bout the good ol' Days
I
know that Heaven doesn't wait
one Day You'll be gone
all I'll have are the stories
from Your past
Let
Me write them down to last and last
Well
They say that My Grandpa
was the Son of a Slave Man
who escaped far into the Indian land
There
He met and fell in love
with My Grandma
from them bones here We are
"Now
Your Grandaddy was a handsome Man
but
My Dad said I was too Young
to take His hand
We
disobeyed and married anyways
born to Us seven strong
Your Grandaddy worked His fingers
to the bone
providing for His Children

till They were grown
I
worked in the fields
when Your Grandaddy took ill
in time God called Him home
later on
four of Our Children
They too were gone
Life
has a way of shaking trees
My childlike ways
slowly creeping up on Me
Take
these words put them in Your heart
treasure them all
for memories tend to fall apart
and
there will be nothing
of where You come from finish to start"

Make a Change

*A*s
I opened the door
He
knocked Me in the head
My
knees hit the floor
thank God I wasn't dead
with pain upon My face
this is what I said
I
knew a young Boy
now a Man
just like You
standing to My feet
I
touched his hand
"God
knows Your heart
He'll understand
take what little I have
material things truly don't last
spare
Me My life is all I ask"
A
hardened voice didn't last long
as He spoke to Me
His
strength was no longer strong

this was God indeed,
"Today
is Your lucky Day,
Old Lady,
'cause
I'm just gonna walk away"
"God Bless You, Son,
The
Lord forgives You
and Just like Jesus
I
do too
this is Your time
let Your past be Your last
and make a change"

MOTHER'S PRAYER

I
can hear you calling
see You falling
but
can't pull You through
not while those drugs got a hold
on You

In
My dreams
You're wasting away
the pain I feel inside
keeps Me in tears night and day

Lord,
don't let the streets
tear Him apart
though
He's a grown Man
let Me hold His heart
if not His hand
'cause
I'm not ready
to say goodbye
can't You see
I'm fighting for His life

I'll
keep on praying
getting down on My knees
Oh,
Lord, I'm begging
asking You please
My Son
bring Him home to Me

OLD PAIR OF SHOES

I
wouldn't cry for having to wear
torn clothes
or
complain when the house was cold
sometimes
We didn't have food
but for one
I'd give it all to Sista
'cause She had none

I
would pray
You never leave Us
like Daddy
always remembering the day
He went away

Sista
and I were playing outside
Miss Johnson
said with tears in her eyes
holding Us tight
God was going to save Our lives

I
didn't understand
till one Sunday morning
outside of town
down by the ol' creek
with no one around
You
got out of the car
not looking back
just walked away
God
was in the midst

I
was not afraid
upon My Sista
a kiss Angels laid
I
love you,
Momma,
We
forgive You
guess You were having a bad day
to have thrown
Us away like an old pair of shoes

MUTHA'S HOUSE

*T*here it lay
Crumbled to ashes
Burned to the ground
Down to its last flame

I embraced the thin woman
Ever so small
Whom I called my mother
With her frail hands
She wiped tears
From her aged face
Crying, "My house, your daddy's place"

It pained my heart
As I watched her dig
Through the soaked pieces of a lifetime
Some things you just can't let go
As she picked up a doll
With cinched hair and a burned face

I could hear her voice
Rising in the midst of a dark smoke,
"I thank God for all he gives
So
If they bum it down
Steal it away and even tear it apart
My precious memories are safe
'Cause I keep them deep within my heart"

MY FATHER

*A*t
least once or twice
I
stare in the mirror
to see Grandma's eyes
My
Mother's cheekbones
born to My face
upon
My lips Grandpa's smile
had found its place
It
took hours
tracing the patterns
that created Me
but
My Father
did not appear
Lord,
where could He be
Was
He in the wind
that dried
tears I cried
while
laying My worries to one side
Or
the silent laughter

My Heart feels
after another World disaster
Had
He become My strength
when I couldn't bear it all
catching
Me before I'd fall
Like
invisible wings
shadowing My shoulders
lifting Me above the pain
of
not seeing His face
nor
the mention of His name
Wherever
You may be,
My Father,
You're a part of Me

NEW HEART

*L*ooking
out the window watching
other Children play
"Baby,
come away from there"
She
constantly heard Me say
I
wish You could understand
then
I'd feel Her heart skip a beat
under the palm of My hand
"Momma,
I just want to run,
try to win a race,
stand
in the rain,
feel the drops upon My face
If
the Bible says
God
loves all the little Children
each Boy and Girl
why
is this happening
doesn't God love Me?"
"Baby,
never doubt God's words

trust and believe
all
that You've said He has heard
there's a plan
with Your heart in His hand
for
You to jump and shout
dance and sing
as
You fall asleep
to the sound
of Your new heartbeat

OLD BLOOD IN NEW VEINS

*I*t
was in the nineteen hundreds
that Daddy and Grandpa
lived the Cowboy way
mending fences to raising cattle
farming and ranching every day
most of their time spent on a saddle
My Brother and I
would practice
roping string around our toes
till
We could rope that ol' fence post
Riding horses
to segregated schools
We'd
tie our horses under the same trees
for their prejudice
didn't matter to them or Me
Seeing
the sweat upon the old Man's back
We
still followed in those same foot tracks
Herding cattle
from the Trina Ranch
in Devine, Texas,
for two young boys was a big deal
twenty-eight miles
to Persalle, Texas,

along dirt roads and open fields
This
blood travels long and deep
through My veins
like
the whispering voice
to look for sick cows
or breaking a horse
I
pray don't ever change

Old Blood in New Veins

*N*ow
My Father
begun a Cowboy life
at six or seven years old
God rest his soul
lived and died
not letting go
Below
King Ranch
to Hollywood Camp
a
hunting Guide I am
from
the rising of the Morning Sun
I
load My dogs
start the truck
the day has just begun
hunting deer to wild hogs
running into
turkeys and black bucks
Ah,
this is the life I love
swimming in a pond
seeing
rattle snakes
eight to ten feet long

I
have no regrets
an adventure
within this heart belongs
White and Red
change of the sand
worth
waking up to this magnificent land
God,
thank You
in Jesus's name
for
these Cowboys old blood in new veins

9/11

$\mathcal{W}$hen
the planes came crashing
sounded like a thunderstorm
on a clear day
while
the fires were burning
felt like the scorching sun
in the month of May

As
tears were falling
it was like a raging river
having its way
pain
in their voices
came crying out
"Lord,
help Me find My Father"
I
heard someone shout,
"Is My Brother in there?"
"God,
let My Mother be elsewhere"

There
would never
no ever
be enough reasons why
hate could cause many people to die

But
it didn't get in the way
of Strangers
becoming Friends
Heroes
held uplifted hands
hearts
joining together
becoming one
that tragic day of 9/11

No Place like Home

*T*hank You,
Mr. Radio Man,
for allowing Me
a chance to reach My Babe
You
see She left Me
this letter saying,
"Dear Momma
I'm
sorry for the way We fought
never thought
this would be the way I'd say goodbye
just can't stay where rules apply
I
can tell You not to worry
I'll be alright
but
knowing You there will be restless night
Everything
about You, Momma, is supposed to be
I love You
signed Me"
Now
She's just My little Girl
rushing to be a Woman
and this will certainly happen in this
fast-paced World
Baby,

You need to slow down
before You become lost
think
about what will be the trade off
Mamas
are gonna be Mamas
disciplining and protecting
ready to hold Your hand
doing the best She can
take it from Me the streets will make You old
sooner then You know
I
have Angels surrounding You
You're never alone
I love You
and there's no place like home

OLD BOOTS UPON MY FEET

I
was a simple Man
did the best I could
No
My life wasn't grand
but
it sure was good
like the one pair of boots
with worn soles
gone through all kinds of weather
bouncing back
like new leather
I
kicked stones, on bad heels
with long hours
My strength
was God's power
I
silently prayed
as I lay My head
readied My boots beside My bed
for a night's rest
to see the Morning Sun
I'm
Ninety-four years old
life for Me ain't done,
Lord,
when My steps are shortened

in these old boots
torn and tattered
Heaven won't wait
a spit shine won't matter
I'll be ready to walk
through those pearly gates
stepping on golden streets
with those old boots upon My feet

PICK ME

$\mathcal{L}$et
Me be the one
You choose today
that steals Your heart away

You
may think I'm too old
just a gem of a pearl
with a heart
aching to be a part
of Your world

I
can't promise there won't be
a few let downs
but
if You choose Me
for Your baby
let Me be Your Child
I'll make Your life worthwhile

Smiles
in the early morning
prayers
before bed
to thank God
for where I'll lay My head

So
don't let fear
keep Me here
unlock this cage
set My wings free
and pick Me

ONE REQUEST

I've
gone to Heaven
God rest My soul
joining loved ones
that left not so long ago
But
after My Birth
through Heaven and Earth
I
have just one request
where My spirit is laid to rest
May
it be upon the grounds
I used to play
till I grew up and moved away
Yes,
Grandaddy and Mutha's land
let My ashes fall
like wild seeds
mixing in the dirt and sand
Drifting
through the trees
to settle upon its changing leaves
like an early Morning dew
That's
where I wanna be
if this one request you grant to Me

REACH

L ord,
I pray rescue Me
Cry
for the lack of food
please feed Me
so
I
may not dig in Your trash
for Yesterday's meal
You see
I'm not some clutter upon Your streets
I
lean on these walls
to shelter Me from the cold
warming My feet
down through My lonely soul
When
I reach out My dirty hand
forgive Me
I'm
still Human try to understand
I
hurt from being trampled on
lift Me
and I'll be on My way
I
stopped wondering
how this all began

once a Veteran
fighting for this great Land
now
You call Me a beggar
even less a Bum
We
are many lost within Ourselves
I'll
take part in the blame
fault
often falls on someone else
it's a crying shame
But
I'm trusting in God
Americans
can find a way
If
We believe in what We preach
Then
let Us lift a helping hand
and reach

Road Trip

I
stole Grandpa
from the old Folk's home
a place I felt He didn't belong
with his hat in His hand
We walked out the door
I
promised Him He wouldn't be back no more
Riding
what seemed like hours
We pulled up to an old farm house
just
like the one Grandpa used to talk about
seemed as empty as could be
We sat under tall oak trees
In
a fish pond We cooled Our weary feet
till a Stranger came about
pointing his rifle at Me
I
apologized told Him what I had done
He saw the gleam in Grandpa's eyes
the smile upon His face
threw up His hands
saying, "Don't forget to close the gate"
Soon
We were back on those old dirt roads
many without names

Grandpa telling stories
some I can still reclaim
Then
silence filled the air
My heart knew He was no longer here
I
felt His spirit
as I whispered in His ear,
"I'm taking You home where You belong"
I
buried Him in a grave next to Grandma's
wrote His name upon Her stone
Family
was angry many were upset
But
I'll never forget
that stolen moment in time
when Grandpa and I took a road trip

Still A Child

*H*ush,
little Girl,
don't tell a soul
are the secret words
that was never told
An
unclean hand
dirtied your pretty dress
a hidden past you've put to rest

Your
all grown up
don't hide your head in shame
Your childlike presence was not to blame
You've emptied your heart
for a brand-new start

Try to let it go
dry your tears
from here on out
refuse to live in fear
silence
you need not hold
don't be afraid, let your story be told

Love
is gentle
in every way a child
sweet and innocent
is still a Child

THAT'S MY MOMMA

I
stood there
knees knocking
legs shaking
My heart skipping a beat
holding Grandpa's hand
so tightly I could hardly breathe
finally the lady
who made Me her baby
stood before Me
at last
no longer an imagination
from My past

I
stole a peek
through the rustic key hole
fearing the old door would squeak
and wake her from her sleep
she was everything
I knew she would be
long thick hair
silky brown skin
she looked just like Me

Right
at that moment
I could hear My Heart say,
"That's My Momma
I'm seeing
if just for today
she belongs to Me"

SUZIE

*S*uzie was my best friend
Till someone took her away
As I sit under the tree
Where we used to play
I can faintly hear her say,
"Don't talk to strangers
They're not your friends
Run, Janie, run
One day you'll understand

"We won't grow old together
Lost pinky promises to be pals
Gone forever
You're just a little girl
Let no one
Steal your perfect world"

Suzie's gone to heaven
Her spirit is with me
When I pray
Protecting, keeping me safe
So no one takes me away

THIS IS MY LIFE

I
was thumbing through the pages
of what I called My life
I
couldn't help but notice
words had been rearranged
like
God and strength
replaced loneliness and pain
in
the section where My tears
smeared shameful blame
it had been erased
I
struggled to understand
till
I saw the fingerprints of his hand
it
was Jesus
picking up the pieces
of My broken heart
putting it back together
leaving out the worthless parts
God
opened My eyes
no
longer afraid to look back
in the Yesterdays gone by

Love
between a Woman and a Man
should survive what is forever
holding to the faith
I'm trusting that it can
Joy
of birth carried no hurt within
Laughter
during a loss
means We'll see each other again
We
have just one
and I believe it's true
Yes
this is My life
but
if You search these words
You'll find a little bit of You

THROUGH THE STORM

I
could see it
hovering above the trees
whispering
as though someone calling Me
I
started running across
miles of open field
till
I came upon this old barn
bare of life
dust weighed down the empty spider webs
above My head
I began to cry,
"Lord,
has this been the place I come to die?"
Boards rattled
over a large hole
a dark cloud settled
blocking the only daylight
struggling to survive
It
was time to pray
before My words rolled off My tongue
this won't last
I
could hear Grandma say,
"From one end to the other

let it pass"
No
longer on this earth
clear was Her words
doors flew open wide
the storm found its way inside
I
saw Her face as I closed My eyes
Cold like a train
trying to cradle Me in its passing
the sound lived up to its name
The wind was strong coming
and softly going
leaving Me and this old barn
standing with no harm
God's so wonderful
to present himself
in the image of Grandma
to see Me through the storm

This Is Not Love

$\mathcal{W}$e
have this knockdown
dragged-out
kind of love affair
I
keep asking Myself
why
am I still here
every time
I
pack My bags
head toward the door
You appear begging Me
like you've done many times before

I
guess that's when
I close My eyes
see
what I want you to be
A
loving Man
with a tender hand holding Me

I
know I'm just living a lie
'cause your eyes say
I
could never be the perfect wife

Lord,
I
don't want to be a casualty
a Woman who never knew
what I could be
If
you say You love Me
then be a better Man
Let
this be the day
You will not raise Your hand
go Our separate ways
listen
to the one above
He sees this is not love

WILL I MAKE IT INTO HEAVEN

"Momma,
do You think
I'll make it into Heaven
when I die
do You know
if Jesus will open the gates
as You get down
on Your knees to pray
could You put in a word
for Me please
Yes
I'm dying
AIDS has taken over Me
never thought I would need
help this way
ever since I was a little Girl
I was taught how to pray
But
right now seems like
I can't find the words to say"
"Daughter,
don't hold back
just give all that's upon Your heart
and let Jesus do his part"
"I
don't wanna spend
what's left of My life alone

I
need Your hugs
want to hold Your hand
enjoy My family and My best Friend
My
biggest fear
is not leaving here
it's wondering if I'll
make it into Heaven"
"Baby,
I've always had answers to the best
I knew how
now this is between You and God
only He knows, My Child"

ABOUT THE AUTHOR

 *B*arbara came from a small town in Texas called Natalia, was raised by her grandparents David and Melissa Haywood. There was not much to do there except go to church, school and ride horses or play sports. Barbara had a wide imagination for life, and writing it down was how she made the town bigger than what it was. Her hobbies were photography, singing, and going off into the pastures to see things that really weren't there. She could get lost in a world; she did not but wanted to belong. That's where her interest in writing began. After spending eighteen years in Natalia, Barbara moved to Oxnard, California, to live with her mother, stepfather, and four Siblings. This was a huge change coming from a little town to a big city. But like everything in life, she learned to adjust. Her mother (Juanita) and stepfather (William Jones) built them around the word of God. Barbara's mother is an evangelist and he was a Preacher, who kept prayer heavy in their house. Lord knows she's had her hardship of disappointments in life and becoming a single mom to Quincy and Samantha, But by the grace of God and prayer, she rose above it all. Her stepfather with his caring ways won her heart over, calling him Dad. He said to Barbara once, "I want to see your poems in your book." It was a wake-up call, though many of her spiral notebooks of poems became heavy from the dust settling upon them. She did nothing until she married her husband Daniel B. Woodson Jr. He had heard and heard so many

poems and readings for funerals, like her dad, he said, "Do something with them, put your dream in your hands," so she did. She is grateful. If she could fall and get back up and see that no matter what the World puts forth, God is greater. Words have a way of saying all the things you wish you could say out loud, telling stories of everyone that can't speak their truth and what their hearts are bursting to tell. Barbara felt she could see in their silent eyes and tell their story, good or bad, with God as her guide who said, "Speak, I say speak…"

CPSIA information can be obtained
at www.ICGtesting.com
Printed in the USA
LVHW030624201119
637819LV00008B/1077/P